DO YOU LOVE YOUR TEAM?

A QUIZ BOOK FOR MAN UTD FANS

Colin Merton

Also from Candescent Press

Coming Nov 2016   Out Now!   Out Now!

Publisher Information

Candescent Press

info@candescentpress.co.uk

www.candescentpress.co.uk

ISBN-13: 978-1469926681

CONTENTS

Welcome & Thank You!!

We donate a large part of our profits on each book to charity – so thanks for buying the book (or go and give the person who bought it a big hug!).

So far we've helped charities working in the areas of Mental Health, Homelessness, Dementia and more. We'll keep going till people stop buying our books, so if you liked the book and want to help, a review would be appreciated!

About the Book

The book is split into nine sections, ranging from Pre-Season Training through to The Cup Final. Each section is a game of two halves!

After every eleven questions you get the questions repeated along with the answers so you can quickly see how well you got on!

We believe all the answers are correct as of October 2016, but if you fancy challenging our knowledge let us know by emailing info@candescentpress.co.uk

1. Pre-season Training

First Half

QUESTIONS

1. Pre-season Training
First Half - QUESTIONS

1. Which player was voted the second best in Europe, in the 1999 Ballon D'or awards?

2. In 1982, which United player became, at the time, the youngest to play at the World Cup Finals?

3. Which brothers played for United in the 1977 FA Cup final?

4. Prior to 2016, how many times had United won the FIFA World Club Cup, and in which years?

5. Three United players were named European Footballer of the Year during the 60s. Who were they, and in which years?

6. United won the 1999 Champions League final by coming from behind to beat Bayern Munich. Who scored Bayern Munich's goal?

7. Which player had a less than "Outstanding" musical career?

8.   Who were Dolly and Daisy?

9.   What shirt number did Eric Cantona wear?

10.   This Northern Irish winger scored 71 times for United. Who was he?

11.   United won the Manchester derby in April 2015 4-2. Can you name United's scorers?

1. Pre-season Training

First Half

ANSWERS

1. Pre-season Training
First Half - ANSWERS

1. Which player was voted the second best in Europe, in the 1999 Ballon D'or awards?
A. *David Beckham - he was in second place behind Rivaldo.*

2. In 1982, which United player became, at the time, the youngest to play at the World Cup Finals?
A. *Norman Whiteside.*

3. Which brothers played for United in the 1977 FA Cup final?
A. *Jimmy and Brian Greenhoff.*

4. Prior to 2016, how many times had United won the FIFA World Club Cup, and in which years?
A. *Just once - in 2008.*

5. Three United players were named European Footballer of the Year during the 60s. Who were they, and in which years?
A. *Denis Law (1964), Bobby Charlton (1966), and George Best (1968).*

6.   United won the 1999 Champions League final by coming from behind to beat Bayern Munich. Who scored Bayern Munich's goal?

A.   *Mario Basler.*

7.   Which player had a less than "Outstanding" musical career?

A.   *Andy (Andrew) Cole. Outstanding was the name of the record he released.*

8.   Who were Dolly and Daisy?

A.   *Gary Pallister and Steve Bruce.*

9.   What shirt number did Eric Cantona wear?

A.   *Seven.*

10.   This Northern Irish winger scored 71 times for United. Who was he?

A.   *Sammy McIlroy.*

11.   United won the Manchester derby in April 2015 4-2. Can you name United's scorers?

A.   *Ashley Young, Marouane Fellaini, Juan Mata and Chris Smalling.*

1. Pre-season Training

Second Half

QUESTIONS

1. Pre-season Training
Second Half - QUESTIONS

12. How many times did Bobby Charlton play for United?

13. Which player won back to back PFA Player of the Year awards in 2006/7 and 2007/8?

14. In which year was Ryan Giggs born?

15. How many Premier League titles had United won by 2016?

16. Which player was known as Jaws?

17. Rio Ferdinand's middle name is Gavin. True or False?

18. In which country was Patrice Evra born?

19. Born in Edinburgh in 1984, this player captained Scotland at the age of 20. Who is he?

20. Gary Bailey ended his playing career at which 'musical' club?

21. Which Scottish architect designed Old Trafford?

22. Which team did United buy Anthony Martial from?

1. Pre-season Training

Second Half

ANSWERS

1. Pre-season Training
Second Half - ANSWERS

12. How many times did Bobby Charlton play for United?
A. *758.*

13. Which player won back to back PFA Player of the Year awards in 2006/7 and 2007/8?
A. *Christiano Ronaldo.*

14. In which year was Ryan Giggs born?
A. *1973.*

15. How many Premier League titles had United won by 2016?
A. *Thirteen.*

16. Which player was known as Jaws?
A. *Joe Jordan.*

17. Rio Ferdinand's middle name is Gavin. True or False?
A. *True.*

18. In which country was Patrice Evra born?
A. *Senegal.*

19. Born in Edinburgh in 1984, this player captained Scotland at the age of 20. Who is he?

A. *Darren Fletcher.*

20. Gary Bailey ended his playing career at which 'musical' club?

A. *Kaizer Chiefs.*

21. Which Scottish architect designed Old Trafford?

A. *Archibald Leach.*

22. Which team did United buy Anthony Martial from?

A. *Monaco.*

2. Friendly Matches

First Half

QUESTIONS

2. Friendly Matches
First Half - QUESTIONS

1. Who is taller? Eric Cantona or Christiano Ronaldo?

2. Which player, who later went on to play for United, won the Ballon D'or in 2001?

3. Which of the United twins, Fabio and Rafael, made his league debut first?

4. Which team did Denis Irwin play for after leaving Manchester United?

5. How old was Edwin van der Sar when he retired?

6. In what year was Patrice Evra born?

7. Which player was Sir Alex talking about when he said, "I used to have a saying that when a player is at his peak, he feels as though he can climb Everest in his slippers. That's what he was like"?

8. Which Chelsea player did Wayne Rooney stamp on, when he was sent off at the 2006 World Cup Finals?

9.   Prior to Alex Ferguson how many Scottish managers had United had since 1900?

10. Against which side did Ryan Giggs make his debut?

11. Which United manager said "The most important difference is that I am training the players, not in the legs, but in the brain, in brain power"?

2. Friendly Matches

First Half

ANSWERS

2. Friendly Matches
First Half - ANSWERS

1. Who is taller? Eric Cantona or Christiano Ronaldo?
A. *Cantona. He's 6'2" and Ronaldo is just 6'1".*

2. Which player, who later went on to play for United, won the Ballon D'or in 2001?
A. *Michael Owen.*

3. Which of the United twins, Fabio and Rafael, made his league debut first?
A. *Rafael - against Newcastle on 17th August 2008.*

4. Which team did Denis Irwin play for after leaving Manchester United?
A. *Wolverhampton Wanderers.*

5. How old was Edwin van der Sar when he retired?
A. *40.*

6. In what year was Patrice Evra born?
A. *1981.*

7. Which player was Sir Alex talking about when he said, "I used to have a saying that when a player is at his peak, he feels as though he can climb Everest in his slippers. That's what he was like"?

A. *Paul Ince.*

8. Which Chelsea player did Wayne Rooney stamp on, when he was sent off at the 2006 World Cup Finals?

A. *Ricardo Carvalho.*

9. Prior to Alex Ferguson how many Scottish managers had United had since 1900?

A. *Five.*

10. Against which side did Ryan Giggs make his debut?

A. *Everton.*

11. Which United manager said "The most important difference is that I am training the players, not in the legs, but in the brain, in brain power"?

A. *Louis van Gaal.*

2. Friendly Matches

Second Half

QUESTIONS

2. Friendly Matches
Second Half - QUESTIONS

12. Which player scored in both the FA Cup and Champions League finals in 1999?

13. Which former United player began his professional career with Auxerre in the 1980s?

14. What was Mark Hughes' nickname?

15. Who said, "It's up to every player to find their home, I found mine at United"?

16. Who holds the record for consecutive appearances in a United shirt?

17. "They say I slept with seven Miss Worlds. I didn't. It was only four. I didn't turn up for the other three." Which player is talking?

18. Which Scottish striker scored two goals for United in the 1963 FA Cup Final?

19. Who beat United in the 1969 European Cup Semi-final?

20. United were originally formed by workers in which industry?

21. United came from two down in the 1979 FA Cup final, only to lose to a goal in the 89th minute. Who were they playing?

22. What was the score in Alex Ferguson's last game as manager?

2. Friendly Matches

Second Half

ANSWERS

2. Friendly Matches
Second Half - ANSWERS

12. Which player scored in both the FA Cup and Champions League finals in 1999?

A. *Teddy Sheringham.*

13. Which former United player began his professional career with Auxerre in the 1980s?

A. *Eric Cantona.*

14. What was Mark Hughes' nickname?

A. *Sparky.*

15. Who said, "It's up to every player to find their home, I found mine at United"?

A. *Ole Gunnar Solskjaer.*

16. Who holds the record for consecutive appearances in a United shirt?

A. *Steve Coppell (206).*

17. "They say I slept with seven Miss Worlds. I didn't. It was only four. I didn't turn up for the other three." Which player is talking?

A. *George Best.*

18. Which Scottish striker scored two goals for United in the 1963 FA Cup Final?

A. *David Herd. (Denis Law also played and scored one goal).*

19. Who beat United in the 1969 European Cup Semi-final?

A. *AC Milan.*

20. United were originally formed by workers in which industry?

A. *The Railway industry.*

21. United came from two down in the 1979 FA Cup final, only to lose to a goal in the 89th minute. Who were they playing?

A. *Arsenal.*

22. What was the score in Alex Ferguson's last game as manager?

A. *It was an astonishing 5-5 draw with West Brom!*

3. The Season Kicks Off

First Half

QUESTIONS

3. The Season Kicks Off
First Half - QUESTIONS

1. What colour shirt did United wear in the 1968 European Cup Final?

2. He made his debut against Torpedo Moscow in 1992, and went on to play for United 602 times. Who was he?

3. In 1940, United had to play a home game at another team's ground, due to damage from a bombing raid. Whose ground was it?

4. Which ex-player had a role in the 1998 film Elizabeth?

5. Who was the first United player to be crowned PFA Player of the Year?

6. Which club did United sign Ruud Van Nistelrooy from in 2001?

7. Which United player won the PFA Player of the Year award for the 1999/2000 season?

8. Which United player was the first ever to be sent off in an FA Cup final?

9. Which player scored a late equaliser in a 1996 UEFA Cup tie against Rotor Volgograd?

10. As of 2016, how many times had United won the League Cup?

11. David De Gea was signed from which Spanish club?

3. The Season Kicks Off

First Half

ANSWERS

3. The Season Kicks Off
First Half - ANSWERS

1. What colour shirt did United wear in the 1968 European Cup Final?

A. *Blue.*

2. He made his debut against Torpedo Moscow in 1992, and went on to play for United 602 times. Who was he?

A. *Gary Neville.*

3. In 1940, United had to play a home game at another team's ground, due to damage from a bombing raid. Whose ground was it?

A. *Stockport County (they played at Man City's ground, Maine Road, later in the war).*

4. Which ex-player had a role in the 1998 film Elizabeth?

A. *Eric Cantona.*

5. Who was the first United player to be crowned PFA Player of the Year?

A. *Mark Hughes in 1989.*

6. Which club did United sign Ruud Van Nistelrooy from in 2001?

A. *PSV Eindhoven.*

7. Which United player won the PFA Player of the Year award for the 1999/2000 season?

A. *Roy Keane.*

8. Which United player was the first ever to be sent off in an FA Cup final?

A. *Kevin Moran (against Everton in 1985).*

9. Which player scored a late equaliser in a 1996 UEFA Cup tie against Rotor Volgograd?

A. *Peter Schmeichel.*

10. As of 2016, how many times had United won the League Cup?

A. *Four.*

11. David De Gea was signed from which Spanish club?

A. *Atlético Madrid.*

3. The Season Kicks Off

Second Half

QUESTIONS

3. The Season Kicks Off
Second Half - QUESTIONS

12. How many English first division titles did United win, prior to the formation of the Premier League?

13. Before playing for United, Kevin Moran won Championship medals at which sport?

14. Two United players have scored a brace (two goals) in European Finals - who were they?

15. Whose statue was erected outside Old Trafford in 1996?

16. Which four United players were in the England squad for the 2002 World Cup Finals?

17. As of 2016, which player held the record for most goals scored in one season, in all competitions?

18. How many League titles did Matt Busby win as United manager?

19. Who did Alex Ferguson want to "knock off their f****** perch"?

20. Which United manager was known as The Doc?

21. Which former United manager once said, "I never comment on referees and I'm not going to break the habit of a lifetime for that prat"?

22. Marcus Rashford scored on his England debut. Which team were England playing?

3. The Season Kicks Off

Second Half

ANSWERS

3. The Season Kicks Off
Second Half - ANSWERS

12. How many English first division titles did United win, prior to the formation of the Premier League?
A. *Seven.*

13. Before playing for United, Kevin Moran won Championship medals at which sport?
A. *Gaelic Football.*

14. Two United players have scored a brace (two goals) in European Finals - who were they?
A. *Bobby Charlton in the 1968 European Cup, and Mark Hughes in the 1991 Cup Winners Cup.*

15. Whose statue was erected outside Old Trafford in 1996?
A. *Matt Busby.*

16. Which four United players were in the England squad for the 2002 World Cup Finals?
A. *David Beckham, Paul Scholes, Nicky Butt and Wes Brown.*

17. As of 2016, which player held the record for most goals scored in one season, in all competitions?
A. *Denis Law (46 in 1963/4).*

18. How many League titles did Matt Busby win as United manager?

A. *Five.*

19. Who did Alex Ferguson want to "knock off their f****** perch"?

A. *Liverpool.*

20. Which United manager was known as The Doc?

A. *Tommy Docherty.*

21. Which former United manager once said, "I never comment on referees and I'm not going to break the habit of a lifetime for that prat"?

A. *Ron Atkinson.*

22. Marcus Rashford scored on his England debut. Which team were England playing?

A. *Australia. England beat them 2-1 at the Stadium of Light, with Rashford scoring in the first five minutes.*

4. The Early Leaders

First Half

QUESTIONS

4. The Early Leaders
First Half - QUESTIONS

1. How many times did goalkeeper Alex Stepney score for United?

2. Andy Cole joined from Newcastle, in a 1995 record transfer. Which player went to Newcastle as part of the deal?

3. At which Argentinian club did Marcos Rojo begin his professional career?

4. Against which team did Ryan Giggs score his first ever United goal?

5. Who is the oldest player to have appeared for United?

6. Who replaced Tommy Docherty as manager?

7. The 1983 FA Cup final ended in a draw, with United winning the replay. Who were United's opponents that year?

8. Who did United beat in the FA Cup Final that formed part of the 1999 treble?

9. Bryan Robson lead United and England throughout the 1980s, what was his nickname?

10. Paul Scholes missed the 1999 Champions League final as he was yellow carded in the semi. True or False?

11. United won the league in 2013 - but who came second?

4. The Early Leaders

First Half

ANSWERS

4. The Early Leaders
First Half - ANSWERS

1. How many times did goalkeeper Alex Stepney score for United?
A. *Twice.*

2. Andy Cole joined from Newcastle, in a 1995 record transfer. Which player went to Newcastle as part of the deal?
A. *Keith Gillespie.*

3. At which Argentinian club did Marcos Rojo begin his professional career?
A. *Estudiantes.*

4. Against which team did Ryan Giggs score his first ever United goal?
A. *Manchester City.*

5. Who is the oldest player to have appeared for United?
A. *Billy Meredith - age 46 in 1921.*

6. Who replaced Tommy Docherty as manager?
A. *Dave Sexton.*

7. The 1983 FA Cup final ended in a draw, with United winning the replay. Who were United's opponents that year?

A. *Brighton and Hove Albion.*

8. Who did United beat in the FA Cup Final that formed part of the 1999 treble?

A. *Newcastle United.*

9. Bryan Robson lead United and England throughout the 1980s, what was his nickname?

A. *Captain Marvel.*

10. Paul Scholes missed the 1999 Champions League final as he was yellow carded in the semi. True or False?

A. *True. Roy Keane also missed out for the same reason.*

11. United won the league in 2013 - but who came second?

A. *Man City came second, a massive 11 points behind.*

4. The Early Leaders

Second Half

QUESTIONS

4. The Early Leaders
Second Half - QUESTIONS

12. Who was known as the Baby Faced Assassin?

13. As of 2016, which United player held the record for most goals league scored in one season?

14. In 2011, from which team did United buy Phil Jones?

15. Which two teams were managed by Bobby Charlton?

16. Who has made the second most appearances for United?

17. What was the last club side that Alex Ferguson managed before United?

18. Which United manager played nearly 400 games in his career, all for the same club, Oxford United.

19. Ole Gunnar Solskjaer scored four goals in record time against Nottingham Forest in 1999. How long did he take? 13 minutes, 16 minutes or 23 minutes?

20. In what year did Matt Busby take over as United manager?

21. Who were United's very first shirt sponsor?

22. Against which team did Paul Pogba make his Premier League debut?

4. The Early Leaders

Second Half

ANSWERS

4. The Early Leaders
Second Half - ANSWERS

12.   Who was known as the Baby Faced Assassin?

A.   *Ole Gunnar Solskjaer.*

13.   As of 2016, which United player held the record for most goals league scored in one season?

A.   *Dennis Viollet (32 in 1959/60).*

14.   In 2011, from which team did United buy Phil Jones?

A.   *Blackburn Rovers.*

15.   Which two teams were managed by Bobby Charlton?

A.   *Preston and Wigan (as a caretaker manager in 1983).*

16.   Who has made the second most appearances for United?

A.   *Sir Bobby Charlton.*

17.   What was the last club side that Alex Ferguson managed before United?

A.   *Aberdeen.*

18.   Which United manager played nearly 400 games in his career, all for the same club, Oxford United.

A.   *Ron Atkinson.*

19. Ole Gunnar Solskjaer scored four goals in record time against Nottingham Forest in 1999. How long did he take? 13 minutes, 16 minutes or 23 minutes?
A.   *13 minutes.*

20. In what year did Matt Busby take over as United manager?
A.   *1945.*

21. Who were United's very first shirt sponsor?
A.   *Sharp Electronics.*

22. Against which team did Paul Pogba make his Premier League debut?
A.   *Stoke City in January 2012. One of just a handful of senior games he played during his first spell with United.*

5. The Busy Xmas Period

First Half

QUESTIONS

5. The Busy Xmas Period
First Half - QUESTIONS

1. From which club did United sign Gordon McQueen?

2. What shirt number was Wayne Rooney given when he joined United?

3. Which player missed the 2009 Champions League final, after being sent off in the semi-final against Arsenal?

4. Who was born first, Jack or Bobby Charlton?

5. Where did Alex Ferguson start his managerial career?

6. Which London club's former home was the venue for United's first FA Cup win?

7. In which year did United first win the English top division?

8. Which team did United beat to win their first FA Cup Final in 1909?

9. In which Scottish city was Alex Ferguson born?

10. Which United Youth Player did the club have to pay a record transfer fee for in 1988?

11. Robin van Persie won the Golden Boot in 2013. How many goals did he score?

5. The Busy Xmas Period

First Half

ANSWERS

5. The Busy Xmas Period
First Half - ANSWERS

1. From which club did United sign Gordon McQueen?

   A. *Leeds United.*

2. What shirt number was Wayne Rooney given when he joined United?

   A. *Eight.*

3. Which player missed the 2009 Champions League final, after being sent off in the semi-final against Arsenal?

   A. *Darren Fletcher.*

4. Who was born first, Jack or Bobby Charlton?

   A. *Jack - he's two years older than Sir Bobby.*

5. Where did Alex Ferguson start his managerial career?

   A. *East Stirlingshire.*

6. Which London club's former home was the venue for United's first FA Cup win?

   A. *Crystal Palace.*

7. In which year did United first win the English top division?

   A. *1908.*

8. Which team did United beat to win their first FA Cup
    Final in 1909?
A. *Bristol City.*

9. In which Scottish city was Alex Ferguson born?
A. *Glasgow.*

10. Which United Youth Player did the club have to pay a
    record transfer fee for in 1988?
A. *Mark Hughes, when he returned to the club in 1988 from
    Barcelona.*

11. Robin van Persie won the Golden Boot in 2013. How
    many goals did he score?
A. *26.*

5. The Busy Xmas Period

Second Half

QUESTIONS

5. The Busy Xmas Period
Second Half - QUESTIONS

12. This long serving full-back signed in 1974. He played 14 times for Scotland. Who was he?

13. Which United captain was born on the 7th November 1978?

14. Which Japanese club did Park Ji-Sung play for? Urawa Red Diamonds or Kyoto Purple Sanga?

15. What was the repetitive title of the United squad's 1983 FA Cup Song?

16. Which United player scored for England in a 1-0 win against Germany, in February 1966.

17. On 25 March 1939, a record 76,952 watched a match at Old Trafford. Which two teams played that day?

18. What were United called before 1902?

19. Which former Chelsea Manager once said, "When Manchester United are at their best I am close to orgasm"?

20. Which veteran rockers teamed up with the United squad for the hit song "Come On You Reds"?

21. Which player, whose United career spanned the 50s, 60s and 70s scored 249 goals for the club?

22. Which club did future United manager José Mourinho first manage?

5. The Busy Xmas Period

Second Half

ANSWERS

5. The Busy Xmas Period
Second Half - ANSWERS

12. This long serving full-back signed in 1974. He played 14 times for Scotland. Who was he?

A. *Arthur Albiston.*

13. Which United captain was born on the 7th November 1978?

A. *Rio Ferdinand.*

14. Which Japanese club did Park Ji-Sung play for? Urawa Red Diamonds or Kyoto Purple Sanga?

A. *Kyoto Purple Sanga.*

15. What was the repetitive title of the United squad's 1983 FA Cup Song?

A. *Glory Glory Man United.*

16. Which United player scored for England in a 1-0 win against Germany, in February 1966.

A. *Nobby Stiles.*

17. On 25 March 1939, a record 76,952 watched a match at Old Trafford. Which two teams played that day?

A. *Wolverhampton Wanderers and Grimsby Town. It was an FA Cup semi-final.*

18.   What were United called before 1902?

A.   *Newton Heath.*

19.   Which former Chelsea Manager once said, "When Manchester United are at their best I am close to orgasm"?

A.   *Gianluca Vialli.*

20.   Which veteran rockers teamed up with the United squad for the hit song "Come On You Reds"?

A.   *Status Quo.*

21.   Which player, whose United career spanned the 50s, 60s and 70s scored 249 goals for the club?

A.   *Bobby Charlton.*

22.   Which club did future United manager José Mourinho first manage?

A.   *Benfica.*

6. Mid-season Madness

First Half

QUESTIONS

6. Mid-season Madness
First Half - QUESTIONS

1. United scored four goals in the 2006 League Cup Final, but who did they beat?

2. When Nobby Stiles left United, which team did he play for next?

3. Sir Alex once said of a player, "If he was an inch taller he'd be the best centre half in Britain. His father is 6ft 2in - I'd check the milkman". Which player was he referring to?

4. In what year was Javier Hernandez born?

5. Who did United play in the very first Charity Shield?

6. What was Paul Ince's nickname?

7. In the season that United won their first English top division title, which team came second?

8. George Best scored a record number of goals in a single match against Northampton in 1970. How many did he score?

9. For which club did United management legend Matt Busby play the most games?

10. How many times have United won the English second division?

11. Which future United player said he turned down a trial with Arsenal when he was 17?

6. Mid-season Madness

First Half

ANSWERS

6. Mid-season Madness
First Half - ANSWERS

1. United scored four goals in the 2006 League Cup Final, but who did they beat?
A. *Wigan Athletic.*

2. When Nobby Stiles left United, which team did he play for next?
A. *Middlesbrough.*

3. Sir Alex once said of a player, "If he was an inch taller he'd be the best centre half in Britain. His father is 6ft 2in - I'd check the milkman". Which player was he referring to?
A. *Gary Neville.*

4. In what year was Javier Hernandez born?
A. *1988.*

5. Who did United play in the very first Charity Shield?
A. *Queens Park Rangers (they drew 1-1).*

6. What was Paul Ince's nickname?
A. *The Guv'nor.*

7. In the season that United won their first English top division title, which team came second?

A. *Aston Villa.*

8. George Best scored a record number of goals in a single match against Northampton in 1970. How many did he score?

A. *Six.*

9. For which club did United management legend Matt Busby play the most games?

A. *Manchester City.*

10. How many times have United won the English second division?

A. *Two.*

11. Which future United player said he turned down a trial with Arsenal when he was 17?

A. *Zlatan Ibrahimovic. Apparenlty "Zlatan doesn't do auditions".*

6. Mid-season Madness

Second Half

QUESTIONS

6. Mid-season Madness
Second Half - QUESTIONS

12. Which player joined United from Torino in 1962?

13. In 2011 Old Trafford set a record attendance for a friendly as United played which US team?

14. Sammy McIlroy was United's top goal scorer in the 1973/4 season. How many goals did he score?

15. Which club did Ron Atkinson manage the season after he was sacked by United?

16. What nationality was Peter Schmeichel?

17. What were the group of young players trained by Matt Busby known as?

18. Prior to becoming Manchester United, Newton Heath had nine International players. They all played for the same country - but, which country was it?

19. From which team did United buy Javier Hernandez?

20. Who became known as the man who "saved Alex Ferguson from the sack", when he scored the winner in an FA Cup tie against Nottingham Forest?

21. How many Premier League titles did Peter Schmeichel win?

22. Which Spanish club did Gary Neville manage in 2015/16?

6. Mid-season Madness

Second Half

ANSWERS

6. Mid-season Madness
Second Half - ANSWERS

12. Which player joined United from Torino in 1962?
A. *Denis Law.*

13. In 2011 Old Trafford set a record attendance for a friendly as United played which US team?
A. *New York Cosmos.*

14. Sammy McIlroy was United's top goal scorer in the 1973/4 season. How many goals did he score?
A. *Just six.*

15. Which club did Ron Atkinson manage the season after he was sacked by United?
A. *West Brom.*

16. What nationality was Peter Schmeichel?
A. *Danish.*

17. What were the group of young players trained by Matt Busby known as?
A. *The Busby Babes.*

18. Prior to becoming Manchester United, Newton Heath had nine International players. They all played for the same country - but, which country was it?
A. *Wales.*

19. From which team did United buy Javier Hernandez?
A. *Chivas de Guadalajara.*

20. Who became known as the man who "saved Alex Ferguson from the sack", when he scored the winner in an FA Cup tie against Nottingham Forest?
A. *Mark Robins (although it has been stated many times since that Ferguson's job was never at risk).*

21. How many Premier League titles did Peter Schmeichel win?
A. *Five.*

22. Which Spanish club did Gary Neville manage in 2015/16?
A. *Valencia.*

7. The Business End

First Half

QUESTIONS

7. The Business End
First Half - QUESTIONS

1. In what year did Nemanja Vidic make his United debut?

2. In 2008, a statue was erected at Old Trafford to celebrate the 40th anniversary of United's first European Cup win. Who is the statue of?

3. How many times have United won the UEFA Cup, forerunner to the Europa League?

4. Who manufactured United's kit during the second half of the 1970s?

5. Which ex-United manager released a song called "It's Christmas – Let's Give Love a Try"?

6. Who scored United's injury time goals in the 1999 Champions League final?

7. Who did United beat to win their first European Cup, in 1968?

8. In which year was the first game at Old Trafford played? 1905, 1908 or 1910?

9. Who did United beat in the 2004 FA Cup final?

10. 70s stars, Sammy McIlroy, Arthur Albiston and Alex Stepney, all made their United debuts playing which club?

11. As of October 2016, four past or present United players have won the European Golden Boy award. Can you name them?

7. The Business End

First Half

ANSWERS

7. The Business End
First Half - ANSWERS

1. In what year did Nemanja Vidic make his United debut?
A. *2006.*

2. In 2008, a statue was erected at Old Trafford to celebrate the 40th anniversary of United's first European Cup win. Who is the statue of?
A. *George Best, Denis Law and Bobby Charlton.*

3. How many times have United won the UEFA Cup, forerunner to the Europa League?
A. *None.*

4. Who manufactured United's kit during the second half of the 1970s?
A. *Admiral.*

5. Which ex-United manager released a song called "It's Christmas – Let's Give Love a Try"?
A. *Ron Atkinson.*

6. Who scored United's injury time goals in the 1999 Champions League final?
A. *Teddy Sheringham and Ole Gunnar Solskaer.*

7. Who did United beat to win their first European Cup, in 1968?

A. *Benfica (4-1).*

8. In which year was the first game at Old Trafford played? 1905, 1908 or 1910?

A. *1910.*

9. Who did United beat in the 2004 FA Cup final?

A. *Millwall.*

10. 70s stars, Sammy McIlroy, Arthur Albiston and Alex Stepney, all made their United debuts playing which club?

A. *Manchester City.*

11. As of October 2016, four past or present United players have won the European Golden Boy award. Can you name them?

A. *Wayne Rooney, Anderson, Paul Pogba and Anthony Martial.*

7. The Business End

Second Half

QUESTIONS

7. The Business End
Second Half - QUESTIONS

12. From which team did United buy Christiano Ronaldo?

13. Who was the last United and England player to be named in a FIFA World Cup All Star team?

14. He scored 150 goals in just 219 appearances. Who was the prolific goalscorer?

15. What nationality is Nemanja Vidic?

16. Who did United play in the last ever FA Cup Semi-final replay?

17. Who was the first player United paid £1,000,000 for?

18. Who is the only United manager who wasn't either English or Scottish?

19. Which ex-United player has won the LMA Manager of the Year award twice?

20. Who has made the most appearances for United?

21. Which Scottish defender once said "99% of players want to play for Manchester United, and the rest are liars"?

22. For how many games was Ryan Giggs manager of United in 2014?

7. The Business End

Second Half

ANSWERS

7. The Business End
Second Half - ANSWERS

12. From which team did United buy Christiano Ronaldo?

A. *Sporting Clube de Portugal (sometimes referred to as Sporting Lisbon).*

13. Who was the last United and England player to be named in a FIFA World Cup All Star team?

A. *Bobby Charlton in 1970.*

14. He scored 150 goals in just 219 appearances. Who was the prolific goalscorer?

A. *Ruud Van Nistelrooy.*

15. What nationality is Nemanja Vidic?

A. *Serbian.*

16. Who did United play in the last ever FA Cup Semi-final replay?

A. *Arsenal.*

17. Who was the first player United paid £1,000,000 for?

A. *Garry Birtles - in 1980.*

18. Who is the only United manager who wasn't either English or Scottish?

A. *Frank O'Farrell - he was Irish.*

19. Which ex-United player has won the LMA Manager of the Year award twice?
A. *Steve Coppell.*

20. Who has made the most appearances for United?
A. *Ryan Giggs.*

21. Which Scottish defender once said "99% of players want to play for Manchester United, and the rest are liars"?
A. *Gordon McQueen.*

22. For how many games was Ryan Giggs manager of United in 2014?
A. *Four. He took over for the last four games of the 2013/14 season after David Moyes was sacked.*

8. Last Day Drama

First Half

QUESTIONS

8. Last Day Drama
First Half - QUESTIONS

1. Which United song featured the lyrics "Because we're up there, cream of the crop, You gotta get up early to keep us from the top!"?

2. Who did United beat in the 1963 FA Cup Final?

3. Which ex-Arsenal manager took over as United's club captain, when Bobby Charlton left the club?

4. As of October 2016, how many times had United paid a fee which broke the British Transfer Record?

5. United only won the European Cup Winners Cup once. Who did they beat?

6. According to Alex Ferguson, who "floated over the ground like a cocker spaniel chasing a piece of silver paper in the wind"?

7. Three goals in five minutes settled the 1977 FA Cup final. Two for United, and one for Liverpool. Name all three scorers.

8. When Peter Schmeichel left United, which club did he sign for?

9. Between 1969 and 2009, only one United player won the Ballon D'or (European Footballer of the Year). Name the player and the year he won.

10. When Norman Whiteside left United, which team did he sign for?

11. David Moyes won his first competitive game as manager of United. Who did he beat in the 2013 Community Shield?

8. Last Day Drama

First Half

ANSWERS

8. Last Day Drama
First Half - ANSWERS

1. Which United song featured the lyrics "Because we're up there, cream of the crop, You gotta get up early to keep us from the top!"?

A. *1995's We're Gonna Do It Again.*

2. Who did United beat in the 1963 FA Cup Final?

A. *Leicester City.*

3. Which ex-Arsenal manager took over as United's club captain, when Bobby Charlton left the club?

A. *George Graham.*

4. As of October 2016, how many times had United paid a fee which broke the British Transfer Record?

A. *Ten.*

5. United only won the European Cup Winners Cup once. Who did they beat?

A. *Barcelona (2-1).*

6. According to Alex Ferguson, who "floated over the ground like a cocker spaniel chasing a piece of silver paper in the wind"?

A. *Ryan Giggs.*

7. Three goals in five minutes settled the 1977 FA Cup final. Two for United, and one for Liverpool. Name all three scorers.

A. *Stuart Pearson and Jimmy Greenhoff for United, Jimmy Case for Liverpool.*

8. When Peter Schmeichel left United, which club did he sign for?

A. *Sporting Clube de Portugal.*

9. Between 1969 and 2009, only one United player won the Ballon D'or (European Footballer of the Year). Name the player and the year he won.

A. *Cristiano Ronaldo in 2008.*

10. When Norman Whiteside left United, which team did he sign for?

A. *Everton.*

11. David Moyes won his first competitive game as manager of United. Who did he beat in the 2013 Community Shield?

A. *Wigan. They qualified having beaten Man City in the FA Cup final earlier in the year.*

8. Last Day Drama

Second Half

QUESTIONS

8. Last Day Drama
Second Half - QUESTIONS

12. Ryan Giggs and Bobby Charlton have played more games for United than any other players - but who is third in the all time appearance list?

13. How many league games did United lose during the 1999 treble season? Three, Four or Five?

14. Who scored the winning goal for United in the 1992 League Cup Final?

15. United broke the British transfer record twice in the Summer of 2001 - which two players did they buy?

16. How many times did United win the FA Cup during the 1990s?

17. Who were United playing when Eric Cantona infamously 'kung-fu' kicked a member of the crowd?

18. Name the three Manchester United players in the 1966 England World Cup squad.

19. How many times did United win the FA Cup during the 1980s?

20. How many United players were in the 2010 World Cup Squad?

21. At which side of Old Trafford is the 'Stretford End'? North, South, East or West?

22. Which United player was a member of the squad who won the 2013 Under 21 European Championship?

8. Last Day Drama

Second Half

ANSWERS

8. Last Day Drama
Second Half - ANSWERS

12. Ryan Giggs and Bobby Charlton have played more games for United than any other players - but who is third in the all time appearance list?

A. *Bill Foulkes.*

13. How many league games did United lose during the 1999 treble season? Three, Four or Five?

A. *Three.*

14. Who scored the winning goal for United in the 1992 League Cup Final?

A. *Brian McClair.*

15. United broke the British transfer record twice in the Summer of 2001 - which two players did they buy?

A. *Ruud van Nistelrooy and Juan Sebastian Veron.*

16. How many times did United win the FA Cup during the 1990s?

A. *Four.*

17. Who were United playing when Eric Cantona infamously 'kung-fu' kicked a member of the crowd?

A. *Crystal Palace.*

18. Name the three Manchester United players in the 1966 England World Cup squad.

A. *Bobby Charlton, Nobby Stiles and John Connelly.*

19. How many times did United win the FA Cup during the 1980s?

A. *Two.*

20. How many United players were in the 2010 World Cup Squad?

A. *Two. Wayne Rooney and Michael Carrick.*

21. At which side of Old Trafford is the 'Stretford End'? North, South, East or West?

A. *West.*

22. Which United player was a member of the squad who won the 2013 Under 21 European Championship?

A. *David De Gea.*

9. The Cup Final
First Half

QUESTIONS

9. The Cup Final
First Half - QUESTIONS

1. In what season did Alex Ferguson win his first league title with United?

2. In what year did Manchester United first win the FA Cup?

3. Which player holds the United record for scoring in the most consecutive matches (ten)?

4. United played in the first Charity Shield in 1908. Where was the match played?

5. With which team did Ole Gunnar Solskjaer start his management career?

6. Which player has scored the most hat-tricks for United?

7. In what year did United win their first European Cup?

8. United shared the 1967 FA Charity Shield with another team, after a 3-3 draw. Which team?

9. Aston Villa, Chelsea, Nottingham Forest, Wolves, Derby, Porto, United. Tommy Docherty managed all but one of these clubs. Which is the odd one out?

10. In which country was ex-United goalkeeper Gary Bailey born?

11. For which team did Jesse Lingard make his senior debut?

9. The Cup Final

First Half

ANSWERS

9. The Cup Final
First Half - ANSWERS

1. In what season did Alex Ferguson win his first league title with United?
A. *1992/3.*

2. In what year did Manchester United first win the FA Cup?
A. *1909.*

3. Which player holds the United record for scoring in the most consecutive matches (ten)?
A. *Ruud van Nistelrooy in 2003.*

4. United played in the first Charity Shield in 1908. Where was the match played?
A. *Stamford Bridge.*

5. With which team did Ole Gunnar Solskjaer start his management career?
A. *Molde (after a stint managing the United reserves).*

6. Which player has scored the most hat-tricks for United?
A. *Denis Law (with 18).*

7. In what year did United win their first European Cup?
A. *1968.*

8. United shared the 1967 FA Charity Shield with another team, after a 3-3 draw. Which team?

A. *Tottenham Hotspur.*

9. Aston Villa, Chelsea, Nottingham Forest, Wolves, Derby, Porto, United. Tommy Docherty managed all but one of these clubs. Which is the odd one out?

A. *Nottingham Forest.*

10. In which country was ex-United goalkeeper Gary Bailey born?

A. *England. He grew up in South Africa but was born in Ipswich.*

11. For which team did Jesse Lingard make his senior debut?

A. *Leicester City. He played for them on loan for a couple of months at the end on 2012.*

9. The Cup Final

Second Half

QUESTIONS

9. The Cup Final
Second Half - QUESTIONS

12. Which United player, and England international, was nicknamed Butch?

13. How many England goals did Bobby Charlton score?

14. Which ex-united player won the Golden Ball at the 2010 World Cup?

15. What nationality is Dimitar Berbatov?

16. In which year did United win the European Cup Winners Cup?

17. In what year were the Da Silva twins born?

18. What nationality is Park Ji-Sung?

19. Which manager called Sir Alex "boss" and "big man", but then served him an awful "paint-stripper" wine?

20. The PFA Player of the Year award has been presented since the early 70s. It's been won by United more times than any other team. As of 2016, which team had the next most winners?

21. When asked about David Beckham, who said, "He can't kick with his left foot, he can't tackle, he can't head the ball and he doesn't score many goals. Apart from that, he's alright"?

22. Who did United beat to win the 2016 FA Cup Final?

9. The Cup Final

Second Half

ANSWERS

9. The Cup Final
Second Half - ANSWERS

12. Which United player, and England international, was nicknamed Butch?

A.   *Ray Wilkins.*

13. How many England goals did Bobby Charlton score?

A.   *49.*

14. Which ex-united player won the Golden Ball at the 2010 World Cup?

A.   *Diego Forlan.*

15. What nationality is Dimitar Berbatov?

A.   *Bulgarian.*

16. In which year did United win the European Cup Winners Cup?

A.   *1991.*

17. In what year were the Da Silva twins born?

A.   *1990.*

18. What nationality is Park Ji-Sung?

A.   *South Korean.*

19. Which manager called Sir Alex "boss" and "big man", but then served him an awful "paint-stripper" wine?

A. *Jose Mourinho.*

20. The PFA Player of the Year award has been presented since the early 70s. It's been won by United more times than any other team. As of 2016, which team had the next most winners?

A. *Liverpool.*

21. When asked about David Beckham, who said, "He can't kick with his left foot, he can't tackle, he can't head the ball and he doesn't score many goals. Apart from that, he's alright"?

A. *George Best.*

22. Who did United beat to win the 2016 FA Cup Final?

A. *They beat Crystal Palace 2-1.*

Printed in Great Britain
by Amazon

35186700R00090